could switch on in the "Leech-gatherer." The world has, in fact, changed, changed utterly, more even than Yeats could imagine, but Brodsky and Heyen are wary of announcing the birth of any "terrible beauty." Only a Himmler is allowed to make such announcements in Heyen's fine poem "Scripture: Himmler on Mercilessness." Following Primo Levi's lead, Heyen and Brodsky would intone "A New Bible," one in which the torments of Job or Christ must be scanned for a logic beyond visible recuperation, since even these agonies have been misunderstood and lethally misapplied by an orgiastic culture.

After what Brodsky calls "the millennial Reich's misappropriation of History" (in "Incarnations of a Pawnbroker"), poetry of this post-Holocaust kind may put us on the verge of rejoining history. Many of the poems in this volume are achingly un-forgettable. (I think especially of Brodsky's "Friday Night Out" and Heyen's "The Children.") They ache with the present that is continuous with the past. Brodsky and Heyen would place us on the edge of a here and now without which tragic con-sciousness is only self-indulgence or nostalgia.

Sanford Budick
Director of the Center for Literary Studies,
The Hebrew University of Jerusalem
Jerusalem, Israel
2 February 1991

Falling From Heaven:
Holocaust Poems of a Jew
and a Gentile

Books By
LOUIS DANIEL BRODSKY

Poetry

Trilogy: A Birth Cycle (1974)
Monday's Child (1975)
The Kingdom of Gewgaw (1976)
Point of Americas II (1976)
Preparing for Incarnations (1976)
La Preciosa (1977)
Stranded in the Land of Transients (1978)
The Uncelebrated Ceremony of Pants Factory Fatso (1978)
Birds in Passage (1980)
Résumé of a Scrapegoat (1980)
Mississippi Vistas: Volume One
    of A Mississippi Trilogy (1983) (1990)
You Can't Go Back, Exactly (1988)
The Thorough Earth (1989)
Four and Twenty Blackbirds Soaring (1989)
Falling from Heaven: Holocaust Poems of a Jew
    and a Gentile (with William Heyen) (1991)

Bibliography (Co-authored with Robert W. Hamblin)

Selections from the William Faulkner Collection of
    Louis Daniel Brodsky: A Descriptive Catalogue (1979)

Faulkner: A Comprehensive Guide to the Brodsky Collection:
    Volume I: The Biobibliography (1982)
    Volume II: The Letters (1984)
    Volume III: The De Gaulle Story (1984)
    Volume IV: Battle Cry (1985)
    Volume V: Manuscripts and Documents (1989)

Country Lawyer and Other Stories for the Screen by
    William Faulkner (1987)

Stallion Road: A Screenplay by William Faulkner (1989)

Biography

William Faulkner, Life Glimpses (1990)

Books by
WILLIAM HEYEN

Poetry

Depth of Field (1970)
Noise in the Trees: Poems and a Memoir (1974)
The Swastika Poems (1977)
Long Island Light: Poems and a Memoir (1979)
The City Parables (1980)
Lord Dragonfly: Five Sequences (1981)
Erika: Poems of the Holocaust (1984)
The Chestnut Rain (1986)
Brockport, New York: Beginning with "And" (1988)
Falling from Heaven: Holocaust Poems of a Jew
   and a Gentile (with Louis Daniel Brodsky) (1991)

Anthologies

A Profile of Theodore Roethke (Editor, 1971)
American Poets in 1976 (Editor, 1976)
The Generation of 2000: Contemporary American Poets
   (Editor, 1984)

Novel

Vic Holyfield and the Class of 1957 (1986)

Falling From Heaven:
Holocaust Poems of a Jew
and a Gentile

by
Louis Daniel Brodsky
and
William Heyen

Louis Daniel Brodsky
12/20/07
St. Louis, MO

TIME BEING BOOKS
POETRY IN SIGHT AND SOUND
Saint Louis, Missouri

Time Being Books
10411 Clayton Road
Saint Louis, Missouri 63131

Time Being Books volumes are printed on acid-free paper, and binding
materials are chosen for strength and durability.

Library of Congress Catalog Card Number: 90-70683

ISBN 1-877770-16-7
ISBN 1-877770-17-5 (pbk.)
ISBN 1-877770-18-3 (tape)
ISBN 1-877770-19-1 (tape & pbk. set)

Designed by Ruth A. Dambach
Southeast Missouri State University
Manufactured in the United States of America

First Edition, First Printing (June 1991)

Acknowledgments

LOUIS DANIEL BRODSKY

The twenty-five poems I have selected for inclusion in this volume have undergone substantial revision, some as a direct result of suggestions offered by William Heyen. All of them have benefited from the close attention to details of fact, punctuation, grammar, orthography, syntax, and style paid by the editorial staff of Time Being Books: Sheri Cornell, Assistant Editor; Jerry Call, Senior Editor, who has supervised the revision of all drafts and the preparation of the final version for publication; and Jane Goldberg, Editor-in-Chief, who has examined each word in every line of all stanzas of my poems in this volume for accuracy and authenticity.

WILLIAM HEYEN

Certain of my poems in this book first appeared in periodicals (*American Poetry Review, The And Review, Colorado Review, Harper's, John Berryman Studies, The Ohio Review, Ontario Review, Poetry East, The Southern Review, Williwaw*) and/or in *The Swastika Poems* (New York: Vanguard Press, 1977), *My Holocaust Songs* (Concord, N.H.: William B. Ewert, 1980), *The Trains* (Worcester, Ma.: Metacom Press, 1981), and *Erika: Poems of the Holocaust* (New York: Vanguard Press, 1984). Grateful acknowledgment is made for permission to reprint.

For

Elie Wiesel

and

Harry James Cargas

HJC	In *Messengers of God*, you remind us that the first death was a murder.
EW	The first death was a murder. Cain killed Abel. . . . The murder of a brother by a brother. That means, again, tragedy. Two men can be brothers, and yet one is a victim and one the murderer of the other. The entire human condition is that bound and enclosed.
HJC	Every murder is a murder of a brother?
EW	Exactly. Every murder means the murder of a brother.
HJC	And as you said elsewhere, it's suicide too.
EW	Every murder means to kill and means to kill oneself. He kills the image that he has of him. I kill myself through him and in him or her. To kill means automatically to be insane. The act of killing is an insane act. It means actually that it is suicide, the death wish.
HJC	And it's also a killing of God, as you say in *A Jew Today*. God is the first victim in every war.
EW	In every war and I said it in *The Accident*, too. When you kill, you kill God.

Harry James Cargas in Conversation with Elie Wiesel

CONTENTS

Falling From Heaven:
Holocaust Poems of a Jew and a Gentile

PART ONE

This Village

Lovesong

The sweetest song I sing is silence.
Can't you hear me whispering in the distance
Or at least read the lyrics of my soaring score
Floating invisibly above you
Like cloud-notes composing themselves
On shimmering vee-staffs
That geese in flight form
Exceeding the speed of sound?

God has chosen me cantor
To chant His wordless reverberations,
Hum the earth's *Kol Nidre*,
Learn all His verses to "World Without End" —
Not just the first and last —
And recite their measures
To anyone who, between breaths,
Listens for Death's deathless echoes.

I'm the song silence sings
Releasing love and praises into my soul.
I'm its mystic spirit
That, becoming ears, eyes, and tongue,
Makes the ineffable audible,
The invisible seen, and allows my voice
Total range over all octaves
Vibrating between Creation and Apocalypse.

Silence and I are eternal.

The Swastika Poems

They appeared, overnight,
on our steps, like frost stars
on our windows, their strict
crooked arms pointing

this way and that, scare-
crows, skeletons, limbs
akimbo. My father
cursed in his other tongue

and scraped them off,
or painted them over.
My mother bit her lips.
This was all a wonder,

and is: how that sign
came to be a star flashing
above our house when I dreamed,
how the star's bone-white light

first ordered me to follow,
how the light began
like the oak's leaves in autumn
to yellow, how the star now

sometimes softens the whole sky
with its twelve sides,
how the pen moves with it,

how the heart beats with it,
how the eyes remember.

For the Time Being

My fifteen-year-old daughter and I
Sit outdoors on the porch,
Side by side on an old depot bench,
Quietly reading,
She, *The Diary of Anne Frank*,
I, *Death of a Salesman.*
Blinded to night's arrival,
We gain insight into signifiers
That have unexpectedly connected us
In a functional oneness
Souls occasionally experience
When least expecting grace
To express unspoken intimacies
They've unknowingly shared
Since long before either was born.

Just like this evening,
While grieving independently
Over gratuitous afflictions of literary others,
We've simultaneously intuited
Our kinship with Anne and Willy
And theirs with each other
Through forebears relating me with my daughter,
Her with her Dad;
The two of us, Jewish waifs,
Cocooned in affluence,
Sitting side by side on a bench
On History's front stoop,
Quietly reading,
Safe from the past and the future —
For the time being.

Men in History

I

Keitel *still* expected the secret weaponry
of deliverance, and maniacal Goering
even *now* angled for power.
Eva Braun, shadowy queen
of this black bower, resigned herself
to long hours of waiting
for cyanide, or one more night's love,

but over the Fuehrer's last days,
as Berlin crumbled above him
and a fine dust seemed
to cloud his bunkers, he moved
divisions of ghosts across maps,
and others around him
kept asking themselves
if this was all a dream.

Shriveled, insubstantial, unreal
even to himself, he walked
with an old peasant's stoop
in a uniform stained by food
dropped by his shaking hands.
Above him, his Reich's burnished eagle
lay in rubble, flew downward into flame.

II

But now it was mid-April,
his birthday, his fifty-sixth
year to heaven,
and since it was his last, and since
he knew, he left for the last time
his shelter and eventual tomb —
sixteen feet of concrete and six of earth —
for the Chancellery's upper rooms,

where walls peeled, drapes were down,
and paintings he'd insisted on
were long since packed away.
A hat lay in an easy chair,
old newspapers haunted the corridors.
This man shook hands, blustered,
passed out signed photographs of himself
framed in silver. Often nostalgia

floated him back twenty years until
his eyes brimmed with tears slashed
away with the back of his hand.

III

Then it was over.
He took his leave, wound
back down to his bunker
to finish the war,
to wait for God to open
the iron gate of the sun
for one more soldier soon
to die. This architect, this

messiah, this man in history
would die just once,
would flame just once into a darkness
far past our spit and curses.
As he said to Albert Speer:
"Believe me, it is easy for me
to end my life. A brief moment
and I'm freed of everything."

➙

IV

Born in Brooklyn of German parents,
I remember lines scratched on our doors,
the crooked swastikas my father cursed
and painted over. And I remember
the *Volksfest* at Franklin Square
on Long Island every summer —
stands of smoked eel, loaves

of dark bread, raffles, shooting galleries,
beer halls, bowling alleys,
boys in *lederhosen*
flooded by an ocean of guttural German
they never learned, or learned to disavow.
I remember hourly parades under the lindens,
the elders' white beards, the sad depths of their eyes.

I remember their talk of the North Sea,
the Rhine of Lorelei, Cologne's
twin towers, the Black Forest, the mountains,
the Hamlin piper who led everyone's children to nowhere.
But I, too, was a child: all those years
there was one word I never heard,
one name never mentioned.

A Sudden Chill

Seated outdoors on his porch
This inordinately warm November afternoon,
He listens to sere leaves,
Still attached to their twigs
Like tongues, whispering distant, gypsy lyrics;
Their diminished fifths and sevenths
Beguile him with perplexing ecstasy
As if their fragile music were a prelude
Not to death, but final silence;
Their hissing voices imitate the friction
Earth makes rotating on its axis.

So focused is he, his ears fail to register
Rake tines scraping concrete sidewalks
As they swoosh debris from lawn to street;
Yelping dogs roaming the neighborhood;
Crows, soaring above oak trees,
Sowing their terribly raucous
Caw-caw-caw seeds;
Sirens of ambulances and fire engines
Speeding to somebody's tragedy;
Lovers strolling and old couples chatting,
Kids skittering past his invisible presence.

Whatever's really compelling his attention,
His senses have inextricably mixed
With the sinister, crisp swishing of brittle clusters
Set astir by the brisk wind
Building minute-to-minute to a dissonant crescendo.
Long before Memory can reach his brain,
His bones recognize Nature's moaning
As Winter's death rattle,
And they know his remaining outdoor hours
Are fading into these notes.
Suddenly he's reciting *Kaddish* for the leaves.

My Holocaust Songs

I

Some split *SS* backbones with axes,
but who can praise them?
Some filed like sheep into the corridors of the swastika,
but who can blame them?
Some found smoke's way to the cosmos,
but who can see them?
Some rose earth's way to grass and pond-pads,
but who can know them?

II

Dead Jew goldpiece in German eye,
dead Jew shovel in German shed,
dead Jew book in German hand,
dead Jew hat on German head,
dead Jew violin in German ear,
dead Jew linen on German skin,
dead Jew blood in German vein,
dead Jew breath in German lung,
dead Jew love in German brain.

III

Break down again, songs, break down
into pure melody, wind's way,
history sung in leaves almost lost,
atoms of singing darkness, the meanings,
the wailing songs of the Holocaust,
themselves dying, returning with spring, the bleeding
notes, break down, break down again, my songs.

Friday Night Out

He's grown so used to living alone,
Living at home,
He never seems to leave anymore
Except on Friday nights,
When he eats at a neighborhood café;
There he sits amidst phantoms
Escaping flickering candle tips
Whose brass sticks are brick chimney stacks
From which he imagines his parents and sister —
Wax-fattened wicks dripping, evaporating —
Lifting into ashen oblivion.

Whether returning early or late
From his one indulgence,
He slips under freshly pressed shrouds,
Pulls up around his neck
Three woolen blankets, summer and winter,
And counts from one million down
Fleeceless Picasso-sheep
Leaping off invisible cliffs
Into Auschwitz pits beside his bed
Before sleep inundates him
With *Zyklon B*-guilements.

For three decades,
He's never abandoned hope
That just one Friday night
He'll glimpse his deported wife, Leah,
Shimmering in a golden, glowing halo
On the front stoop of his dreams,
Greeting him home, again.

Children's Poem: This Village

For Louis Daniel Brodsky

Many orphans from the camps of Europe settled
in this village in Israel.
They studied in school, played, worked the orchards,

but even ten years after the *Shoah*,
they buried bread in hiding places
in their living quarters. Thus

this village thrived but suffered from mice
fattening on bread hidden under mattresses,
in cracks and holes,

beneath floorboards, behind walls,
for who could believe, day after day, there would be bread,
except the mice? —

these kept faith in the children, and waxed.
In this village, the ravenous dead still
gleam in mice eyes.

The Ashkeeper

His birth certificate specifically states
Gender, Race, Place, and *Date*
As male Caucasian,
Jewish Hospital — St. Louis,
April 17, 1941;
And yet, to this day,
His deepest reservations dictate otherwise,
Assail him with misgivings
As if he were an adopted child
Waiting his entire lifetime
For parents, siblings, or distant relatives
To restore his original name.
Some nights, squirming on his belly
Beneath barbed-wire sleep
Tightly stretched between waking and dreams,
He envisions floodlights scanning a camp;
Their crisscross reiterations
Stimulate his rapid eye movements to a blur
Through which he finally escapes
Into a forest beyond Memory's outskirts.

As it disappears, he glimpses back;
Eyes behind an unrecognizable voice
Quavering inside his restive mind
Read and speak a name on the compound gate:
          — O S W I E C I M —
Repeating its three bleak syllables
All the way home from spectral shadows
Through daybreak into consciousness,
He hears his stiff bones disintegrating,
Feels his flaming bowels
And emaciated stomach raging silently,
Smells ubiquitous odors of conflagrant flesh,

                    * * *

And finally realizes what he's always suspicioned:
He was born in Auschwitz,
Not St. Louis,
Warmed in an oven, not an incubator;
Not even a Jew, but God's orphan
Doomed to spend his earthly existence
Fleeing nightly, searching by day
For every person lost in the Holocaust.

The Dead

A survivor, years later, allowed himself to wonder
where the dead were,
all those hanged from beams in their own barns,

or slaughtered against walls,

or herded to their own orchards, shot into ditches,
or starved in cattlecars to camps,
who screamed for God in the agony showers,

who burned their ways into graves in the empty sky. . . .

But then, at last, he saw one, one thin woman in a cloud
in a blue dress wisping away from her,
dress he'd bought her fifty years before.

"*There* you are," he said,

"there," and "there," as others appeared from the west
in bursts of sunlight and cloud,
whole families of them, streets and villages of them,

cities of them, clothed in vapor, returned

by rails of sunlight, by sweeps of cloud, in carriages
of burnished cloud.
He kept waving, kept crying out,

"Here, here I am, *here*,"

but as for them, they sailed over his head, horizon
to horizon, for the rest of his life,
doing all they possibly could — forming, eddying,

obeying the wind.

PART TWO
The Winnowing

To a Distant Land

Over the desolate years,
As a child of parents who died in the camps,
He watched documentaries, read diaries,
And listened to survivors describe ghetto life
During Germany's Jew-scourge.
His inquiries, disorganized and desultory,
Entered into with tremulous curiosity,
Have persisted, actually escalated
These past three years.

He's tried to fathom the cryptic connection
Between Now and Then, Himself and Them, —
Those broken souls
Witnessing gratuitously vicious "Aktions"
Shoving wife and son into one cattle car,
Father, daughter, and grandmother into another;
Those misbegotten spirits —
Fragile families like his,
Decimated by forces hysterical, insane:

Adultery's train streaking past,
Neither he nor Rachel able to slow it,
Leap, and escape into a hallucinatory forest
To hide from swastika-snakes
Until old betrayals might subside,
Wounds from marital genocide
Diminish to disillusionment,
That they might sneak back to the ghetto
To finish out their fractured lives.

Today these converging fates
Leach into the pits of his eyes; he cries
As the car deporting his children and wife
To a distant land for Chanukah
Disappears into a smoky blur,
Stranding him amidst brittle leaves
Littering the front yard of the house
To which they'll never return.
Mortified, he waits to board Death's next freight.

Kotov

Ivan Ivanovitch Kotov, short of speech,
clarity drifting away to mindlessness —
Kotov of stutter and suddenly empty eyes —
only Kotov, in all Russia, of all those locked inside,
survived the *dushegubka*,
the murder wagon, the gas van. Only Kotov,

pushed with his new bride
into the seatless seven-ton gray truck,
stood on that grated floor, and lived. Only Kotov,
pressed together with fifty others, would wake
in the ditch of dead, half buried, and crawl away.
He'd smelled gas, torn off one sleeve,
soaked it in his urine, covered nose and mouth,

lost consciousness, and lived, waking
in a pit of bodies somewhere outside of Krasnodar.
His wife? — he could not find her.
Except for the dead, he was alone. . . .
He stood up, staggered and groped through fields
back to the city, where he hid until the end.

Only Kotov, saved by his own brain and urine, woke
from that wedding in the death van,
in Russia, in the time of that German invention,
the windowless seven-ton gray *dushegubka*.

Lovers' Last Evening in the Warsaw Ghetto

Like a painter decorating a china plate,
My tongue's brush tip
Memorizes each crease of your semen-sweetened belly
As it rims your navel,
Shading in your Rubenesque flesh
With invisibly dripping blood-blue hues
Of mystic wisteria and erika.

My wet lips, like mimesis-geese
Flying southerly down northern corridors
In a formation resembling Love's V,
Seek refuge along your warm shores,
Where once more, just once,
They might bring you to orgasm
Before soaring easterly out of time.

Lying side by pulsating side
In an open grave
Dug out of ageless silence,
We whisper gentle threnodies
Men and women of Masada and Lidice spoke
Seizing their last, lucid evocations of hope
Without ever really knowing so.

Tonight, partaking of pleasure's cadences,
We devote our anonymous lives
To these few, fleet moments possessing us,
Believing we can stall, evanescently,
Time's Kafkaesque Gestapo
We know, come morning,
Will traduce us at gunpoint

And goose-step us nude
From Destiny's westernmost railhead
To shower rooms for lice disinfection;
But not before measuring us
And dressing us in *Zyklon B* nightshirts
For lullaby and "lights out"
In flames of an entire race's *Yahrzeit* candle.

➜

For these precious hours left us,
You and I *must* suppress
Intimations of earthly extermination
And rest contentedly in naked embrace,
Your palpitating breasts pressed to my chest,
My penis, itself a blessed Torah,
Nestled in your dark Ark, eternally sealed.

The Lice Boy of Belsen

Hanna tells of a boy infested with lice
eating their way under his skin,
into his eyelids, his bony chest black with them.

His parents dead, his brother and sister afraid
even to be near him, he begs for space
from one tier to the next.

No use. He is finished this morning,
his corpse a susurrus of fleas and lice.
Hanna says there are thousands of such cases.

This was January 1945, just months from liberation
from the ferocity of winter insects to which,
in whispers, he now testifies, the lice boy of Belsen.

The Winnowing: Warsaw Ghetto, 1943

Cut loose from all moorings —
Grocery-store job,
Wife and two porcelain-doll children,
Strict affiliation
With his Orthodox Jewish congregation,
And permanent address
To which tax-assessment notices
And minute-to-minute obituaries can be sent —
He stutters from second to day to month,
Feckless, half-deaf, expressionless,
Lacking the slightest desire for a nexus
Between idle thoughts and vital deeds
Or an exit from Death's net.

He's no Piers Plowman
Or Pilgrim progressing through bogs and sloughs,
But rather an unsynagogued Jew
Gratuitously bitten
By inescapably ubiquitous swastika-snakes,
Whose crooked-cross shapes lay coiled
Or slither over paths he takes
From shafts in his feces-reeking tenement
To venomous fences and back.
Eventually, he knows, they're going to send him
From ghetto to abyss, Auschwitz.
Right now, he wonders not *what* to do,
But *how* to keep from doing it.

Sunflowers

I

I have six rows this year,
some heads as far from ground, for now, as mine,
some only shoulder-high
but still purposeful in their beauty and seeds.

When wind sways them,
I hear in their leaves that green
enduring wordlessness.
They follow the sun to share and witness.

What, then, is my place with them here?
Lord, when I pray to You for signs from sunflowers,
I am answered only by my own tricks and cleverness.

Let them, and You, be true,
though a hundred scythes hover ready
for every head among us
bowed in prayer for communion with sunflowers.

II

I potted a six-inch seedling, gave it to my friend.
He is a survivor, wants to emulate stone
in its mute power to shrug and withstand.

Tied to a drainpipe outside his apartment,
it leans down to him like someone he knew,
petal corolla-curls of yellow hair,
roots in the tunnels of Warsaw.

While I confer with my own sunflowers on transcendence,
saving seeds for the next planting,
my friend confirms his past in the plant's dying.

Still, it keeps him company I cannot give him.
I've seen him stand beside it, look up into it
as though listening, then nod, and walk away,
for they seem meant for one another, survivor and sunflower,

to shape an intricate despair. No prayer here,
just water making invisible way
from root-veins to petals, and petals falling,
my friend sweeping seed and bits of autumn hair.

III

Much time has passed, if any.
My young plants have not yet grown their heads,
but follow their sun across the sky, twisting
in their leaves, and so will I, and you with me, maybe,

until that fullness:
the dead wait there in our future
at the end of every summer. The sunflowers
somehow know where they will be, and for how long

we'll remember. Each year, faces begin to form
in empty air above them, growing
clearer by the hour.

Bert Jacobs, Furrier

He wakes up at 5 a.m.,
Regularly as a carved cuckoo
Flapping out at intervals
Through the doors of a Black Forest clock.

Demons chew on his dreams
As fast as his brain manufactures them;
They'll possess it, lobes, stem, and all,
If he doesn't keep three steps ahead.

This Saturday morning,
He stirs two hours earlier than usual;
Death's insects squirm on his flesh, —
Worms, vermin, maggots, and lice —

Burrowing into feverishly sweating pores,
Craniofacial and urogenital orifices.
Premonitory forces
Have routed him out of bed,

Set him groping for gold-rimmed spectacles
He needs to differentiate shapes
From shadowy voids
And discriminate between friend and foe.

He knows the rest of his future
Depends on how expeditiously
He can persuade someone, anyone,
To secret him to the next station

Along the underground railroad he uses
To elude Sleep's elite *SS*
He still sees and hears nightly,
Forty years after fleeing Lodz ghetto.

A Professor of Mathematics

I

As the Nazis entered the ghetto,
we tried to hide the children —
this was Bialystok, winter, 1943.

We tried drugs to make the children sleep
through the shouts and fear
penetrating to their hiding places.

Baziunia, four years old, whimpered in her bureau.
The closest, a professor of mathematics,
pressed down on her neck — surely,

he wished only to save her. I buried her
in the garden under that room.
Her mother lifted the body through a window.

"Maybe she is still alive," the mother said,
but no, under her lids the child was dead.

I remember a mild and moonlit winter night,
but the soil was hard,
it was difficult to dig.

II

When the Nazis found the children —
Treblinka. This was Bialystok-Ghetto,
Poland, winter, 1943.

What sleep-drugs we had were for them,
to quiet them in their hiding places
when the Nazis came shouting and looking,

but the drugs were often too strong,
or too weak. Baziunia, four years old,
began to cry in her bureau drawer. Closest,

I angled my hand in to comfort her,
to quiet her,
but pressed too hard.

Later, mother passed daughter's body
through a window to the garden below,

to the moonlit frozen Bialystok-Ghetto soil
wherein the Nazis never found her,
will never find her.

Liberation from Buchenwald

He awakens at 5:00 a.m.;
Although early, it's too late
For his obscure dreams
To alert consciousness to his metamorphosis;
They retreat into Sleep's forest
Like squirrels scurrying behind trees
As a ghostly shape approaches,
Rushes past, and escapes its own shadow.

He emerges from an oneiric furnace
Up whose stack he's volitionlessly floated
Like memory-ashes issuing from chimneys:
Arms with blue, tattooed numerals,
Twisted gruel spoons,
Striped uniforms, worn-out sandals.
Peering through two million pairs of glasses,
He focuses his diminished vision,

Inspects his warped face in a mirror
For ghetto-etched reflections.
Vaguely he recognizes the corpse gazing back
As that Specter he'd met on the road
Who, begging directions to a mass grave,
Would detain him just enough
To throw him incorrectably out of step
The rest of his snowy march home.

Riddle

From Belsen a crate of gold teeth,
from Dachau a mountain of shoes,
from Auschwitz a skin lampshade.
Who killed the Jews?

Not I, cries the typist,
not I, cries the engineer,
not I, cries Adolf Eichmann,
not I, cries Albert Speer.

My friend Fritz Nova lost his father —
a petty official had to choose.
My friend Lou Abrahms lost his brother.
Who killed the Jews?

David Nova swallowed gas,
Hyman Abrahms was beaten and starved.
Some men signed their papers,
and some stood guard,

and some herded them in,
and some dropped the pellets,
and some spread the ashes,
and some hosed the walls,

and some planted the wheat,
and some poured the steel,
and some cleared the rails,
and some raised the cattle.

Some smelled the smoke,
some just heard the news.
Were they Germans? Were they Nazis?
Were they human? Who killed the Jews?

The stars will remember the gold,
the sun will remember the shoes,
the moon will remember the skin.
But who killed the Jews?

PART THREE

Christian Prayer and *Kaddish*

The Baron's Tour

Gaze down at the Rhine.
I remember it red
with Roman blood.
We have always lived in this castle.

This is the room of trophies:
deer, griffin, boar, bear,
the long hair
and leathery scalp of a chinawoman.
Dragon, wolf, lampshade of jewskin.
We have always lived in this castle.

At the base of this stair, a door
opens to the Fuehrer's chamber.
In its center stand
candelabras of eternal flames.

We have thought to leave here,
but the labyrinthine passages,
the sheer plunge to the river,
the stones that have come to caress us . . .

This is the hall once lined
by hearts impaled on pikes.
These are the stair rails
of russian bone.
This is the turret
where the books are burned.

Come, see where kings entered
the grained wood of the oak bed
where you will sleep tonight.
One said he'd dreamed

of his whole courtyard filled with heads
whose eyes mirrored
fields inside of fields inside
of fields forever.
We have always
lived in this castle.

Kristallnacht, **9 November 1938**

> *Ye shall keep My sabbaths, and reverence*
> *My sanctuary: I am the Lord.*
> — Leviticus 26:2

While walking the ten blocks from his house,
He wonders why tonight seems so different.
After all, he's attended synagogue
On this same hit-and-miss basis three decades
With the devoted complacence of a soul
Who, although nominally Jewish,
Has convinced himself his hooked nose,
Furrowed brow, and beady eyes
Have nurtured, not stifled, his assimilation
Into the Teutonic *Zeitgeist,*
Believing even his ethnic dialect,
Composed of High Germanic inflections,
Has in no way exposed his Yiddish mother tongue.

Pressing into the crowded synagogue
To register his presence as a "community leader,"
He muses on why this *Shabbat*
He's sweating so profusely
Under his vested, serge suit.
Is his crotch wet from the steam heat
Or from listening to the rabbi's homily
And exhortations for peace,
His readings from Exodus about God's mercy
And preoccupation with forgiveness,
The *Shema* and *Kaddish* he mumbles by rote?
Why does he respond with such edgy gestures
Amidst people he doesn't even recognize,

Who often see him seated at his desk
Behind a glass partition
As if rigor mortis has set in,
His back to their routine transactions
Over which, as Chief Officer
Of Leipzig's most prestigious bank, he presides?
What's so different about this night
That makes him feel empty,
Intimidated by a sense of vulnerability,
Invaded by wayward premonitions
That his position might not be quite as secure
Or his physical safety as inviolable
As he's always assumed?

Taking in the meek, contrite faces
Of men *dovening* in humbleness
Under weightless yarmulkes and tallisim,
And women silently praying in galleries
(Children conspicuously missing),
He realizes indefensibly
He's indistinguishable from the rest of them
To gangs of youthful hooligans and brutes
Wielding truncheons, pacing outside the gates
Like cougars in zoo cages: Jew baiters!
He intuits, for the very first time
Since becoming bank director,
His citizenship has been a self-delusion.

Suddenly he's caught in a shower of crashing glass.
This sacred house of worship is a *Sheol*
From which no one can escape;
Hordes are boarding doors,
Hurling rocks, rotten fish,
And flaming, gas-filled bottles.
He twitches toward a shattered window,
Lunges, and is impaled on a stained-glass shard.
Stupefied, he moans aloud,
Then, in resignation not to Death, but God,
Cries, "Why's this happening to me?
Why have You forsaken me
So mercilessly?"

In a raspy, gasping spasm,
Blood splattering his silk dress shirt
And three-piece, worsted-wool suit,
He plunges ten feet to the *Judengasse.*
Lapsing from consciousness,
A sad, sweet, compassionate perplexity
Infusing his Semitic eyes and lips,
He's unexpectedly visited with ecstasy
Wisdom bestows on those who transcend knowing
Through inspiration or sheer volition
And achieve ultimate assimilation.
In a flash, he enters Memory intact —
A Jew, at last!

Sonnet and Haiku:
Forms from the Reich University

I

"A junior doctor should . . .
if possible, establish the origin,
date of birth,
and other particulars. . . .
After the killing of the Jew,
the head of whom
must not be damaged,
he separates the head
from the body and sends it
to the appointed place
in a specially prepared
and well-sealed
iron cannister filled
with preservative." . . .

II

This
cannister
of words —
Judaism
suspended
in formal-
dehyde.

Sonderkommando

He pads out onto the front porch
Into April's yawning dawn.
His dazed gaze descends
Through blurry spaces in blooming verdure,
Snags on mazy hallucinations.
Sinking to his unmowed lawn,
He gropes on all fours among uneven tufts

As though trying to gather up
All the grass seed he'd broadcasted last week
Or exterminate colonizing ants
Threatening to transport him.
Without noticing neighbors slowing in cars
On their way to work or gawking from the sidewalk
Buffering him from their world,

He continues his hysterical combing.
Suddenly he uncovers one bone,
Then a second, then hundreds, thousands
He recalls having buried decades ago.
Oblivious of witnesses to his animality,
He starts sniffing, licking, gnawing them,
Foaming from their sickening, cyanic taste.

Poem Touching the Gestapo

> *Behind the apparently iron front of Teutonic*
> *organization, there was a sort of willed chaos.*
> — Edward Crankshaw

> *The system of administration* [at Auschwitz] *was*
> *completely without logic. It was stupefying to*
> *see how little the orders which followed one*
> *another had in common. This was only partly due*
> *to negligence.*
> — Olga Lengyel

You now, you in the next century, and the next,
hear what you'll almost remember,
see into photos where he still stands, Himmler,
whose round and puffy face concealed visions,

cortege of the condemned winding toward Birkenau,

and how to preserve Jews' heads in hermetically sealed tins,

der Ritter, knight, *treuer Heinrich*,

visions of death's head returning in Reich's light,
the Aryan skull ascending the misformed skull of the beast,
the Jew, Gypsy, lunatic, Slav, syphilitic, homosexual,
ravens and wolves, the Blood Flag, composer Wagner
whose heart went out to frogs, who, like Martin Luther,
wanted to drive Jews "like mad dogs out of the land,"

Heydrich dead but given Lidice,
Mengele injecting dye into Jewish eyes —
Ist das die deutsche Kultur? —
this vomit at last this last
cleansing and an end to it,
if it is possible, if I will it now,

Lebensborn stud farms, *Rassenschande, Protocols*
of the Elders of Zion, SS dancing in nuns' clothes,

→

Otto Ohlendorf, who left his Berlin desk to command
Einsatsgruppe D and roam the East killing
one million undesirables in less than two years' time,

lamenting the mental strain on his men,
the stench of inadequate graves,
corpses that fouled themselves in the gas vans,

the graves rupturing, backs, backs of heads, limbs
above ground as they are here, if I will it now,

the day-in, day-out shootings of Jews, some attractive,
brave, even intelligent, but to be dealt with
in strict military order, not like at Treblinka where
gas chambers were too small, and converted gas vans' engines
sometimes wouldn't start, the thousands already
packed into the showers for history,

their hands up so more would fit, and smaller children
thrown in at the space left at the top,
and we knew they were all dead, said Hoess of Auschwitz,
when the screaming stopped,

Endlösung, Edelweiss, Lebensraum, Mussulmen, Zyklon B,

"and his large blue eyes like stars," as Goebbels wrote,
and the Fuehrer's films of conspirators on meathooks,

we cannot keep it all, an end to it,
visions of loyal Heinrich, what engineer Grabe saw at Dubno,
he and two postmen allowed to watch, the vans arriving,
a father holding his boy and pointing to that sky,
explaining something, when the *SS* shouted and counted off
twenty more or less and pushed them behind the earth mound,

Stahlhelm, Horst Wessel, Goering in a toga at *Karinhalle*,
redbeard Barbarossa rising,

that father and son, and the sister remembered by Grabe
as pointing to herself, slim girl with black hair,
and saying, "twenty-three years old,"
as Grabe behind the mound saw a tremendous grave,

the holy orders of the *SS*, Lorelei, the Reichstag fire,
Befehl ist Befehl, Anne Frank in Belsen, jackboots, Krupp,

bodies wedged together tightly on top of one another,
some still moving, lifting arms to show life,

the pit two-thirds full, maybe a thousand dead,
the German who did the shooting sitting at the edge,
his gun on his knees, and he's smoking a cigarette,
as more naked victims descend steps cut in the pit's clay,
clamber over the heads of those already dead there,
and lay themselves down. Grabe heard some speak
in low voice, . . . listen . . .
before the shooting, the twitching, the spurting blood,

competition for the highest extermination counts,
flesh sometimes splashed on field reports,
seldom time even to save skulls with perfect teeth
for perfect paperweights,

his will be done, and kill them, something deeper dying,
but kill them, cognac and nightmares but kill them,
Eichmann's "units," the visions, the trenches
angled with ditches to drain off the human fat,

the twins and dwarfs, the dissidents *aus Nacht und Nebel*,

Professor Dr. Hans Kramer of the University of Münster
who stood on a platform to channel new arrivals —
gas chamber, forced labor, gas chamber — and later,
in special action, saw live women and children thrown into pits
and soaked with gasoline and set on fire —

→

Kramer, a doctor, who kept a diary filled with
"excellent lunch: tomato soup, half a hen with
potatoes and red cabbage, sweets and marvellous vanilla ice,"
while trains kept coming, families with
photograph albums falling out of the cars, the books
of the camps and prisons, the albums imprinting the air,
as here, we close our eyes, and the rain falling from photos
onto the earth, dried in the sun and raining again,
no way to them now but this way, willed chaos,

visions deeper in time than even the graves of the murdered
daughter who tells us her age,
in the round face of the man with glasses and weak chin,
Himmler, *Geheime Staats Polizei*, twisting his snake ring,

as now the millions approach, these trucks arriving with more,
these trains arriving with more, from *Prinz Albrecht Strasse*,
from the mental strain on Ohlendorf's men,
from the ravine at Babi Yar, from the future,
from the pond at Auschwitz and the clouds of ash,
from numberless mass graves where Xian prayer and *Kaddish*
now slow into undersong, O Deutschland, my soul, this soil
resettled forever here, remembered, poem touching the Gestapo,
the families, the children, the visions,
the visions . . .

Himmler at Auschwitz, 1942

A dim image of Heinrich Himmler
Simmers on Imagination's back burner:
He stands at a safe distance
Just in front of Auschwitz's newly finished
Disinfection facility;

Standing at histrionic attention
In his spit-shined jackboots,
SS uniform, cap with patinous brim,
Engraved dress revolver decorating his hip
Like icing on a wedding cake;

Standing statuesquely
With an inscrutable expression,
Waiting for the first thousand victims
To emerge from the very first "Special Aktion,"
Waiting with the patience of Job;

Standing, as low moaning
Slowly metamorphoses into shrill bellowing
That sifts through hastily nailed boards
And lifts in a sick-sweet mixture
Of hysterical syllables and cataleptic gas;

Standing rigidly, gold-rimmed glasses
Focusing to a higher power his myopic eyes
On the montage of choked, naked humans
Being rolled away in coal cars,
Heaved into open pits along the track,

Covered with lime, and left festering
While less fortunate deportees
Sporting Star-of-David patches
Continue backtracking to load the rest,
Freshly sprayed with insecticide;

➜

Standing in astonished admiration
Even after the last corpse has been dispatched,
As though his boots were glued to the earth,
No member of his staff
Daring to make the slightest move to disperse

Despite nausea each can almost hear
Gnawing his gurgling bowels,
Or willing to inform this man of vision,
This mastermind of the Third Reich,
Who promises to purge Germany

Of Jew-vermin, Gypsies, and sexual perverts,
That this initial supply has run dry,
The next freight-train load
Not scheduled to arrive
From the Russian front for two days yet;

Standing like Christ being shown
The glorious Kingdoms of the world
As if from God's throne;
Standing in dazed amazement, reverential,
Contemplating the colossal possibilities of his revelation.

Scripture: Himmler on Mercilessness

(to his *SS* at Poznan, Poland, 4 October 1943)

To speak it is one thing, to practice it another:
not merely imagine, but commit extinction,

commit it mercilessly —

but remain decent: this has made us hard,
this glorious page in our history

that never shall be written. . . .

Should Germany need a tank ditch,
he shall have it, though ten thousand Russian women

perish from exhaustion. . . .

Mercilessness. To carry this through. Glorious.
Mercilessness. Glory. For Germany. We, the *SS*

risen into the power of mercilessness.

Lipizzaner Fantasies of an *SS* Officer

Fantasies prance across the sawdusty floor
Of my brain's three-ring arena
Like a touring team of Austrian Lipizzaners
Executing antic goose steps
Before an audience subdued in awed amazement:

First, as ghostly panzer divisions
Doing dressage maneuvers
Across a map of North Africa
Hung from a crumbling bunker ceiling
Beneath Berlin's upheaved yeshivas and synagogues,

They clip and clop on greaseless tracks
Toward the unsupportable fortification
Where my bivouacked dreams
Have entrenched against the enemy, Nightmare,
To hold Sleep's strategic oasis;

Then, they scurry and lurch past my eyes
Like red-hot swastika-wheels
Vibrating boxcars into violent pitching,
Atop which even rodeo riders
Couldn't stay ten seconds;

Finally as *Sonderzüge* hauling human cattle
For rendering at Nazi-operated
Meat-packing factories — Sachsenhausen,
Mauthausen, Auschwitz-Birkenau —
They arrive at my inner ears' depots

Where numb, slumberous *Kapos* and clerks
Wait to process endless tens,
Hundreds, and thousands of thousands
Before ordering them to disinfection showers
Or moribund work crews

Assigned to carpenter crucifixes
And lay tracks along platforms in the Terminal
Where Europe's Torahtrains
Disgorge History's unfortunate cargo
In a gasping mass of black ash and smoke.

Every restive a.m.,
My nose detects those offensive odors —
Coal raging in locomotive maws
Indistinguishable from flesh
Crackling, like bacon, in Topf ovens —

As though the scrofulous stench I sense
Were emanating from chimneys
Surrounding my sweat-filled pillow,
Chimneys shaped like these Mannheim buildings
Drenching my windows in almond halos.

Why such disdainful hallucinations
Intrude on recuperative rest
Remains unexplained. I suspicion this:
Their intransigent danses macabres,
Gothic dressage, spectral quadrilles,

Choreographed with rigid precision,
Must be diabolically inspired
By the Four Horsemen of the Apocalypse,
Who perform nightly in my dreams
While I applaud. *Sieg Heil! Sieg Heil!*

"Canada"

Across landscapes here now forever beyond innocence, the Jews in their sealed torahtrains. Hiding in luggage among cookingware and clothes, these words of their lost languages: this little lucky hearth's cricket "beauty," (how beautiful the crimson sunset), this mouse "hope," curled in a cello among spools of wool (a bluesweater for Sarah by next winter), "tradition" tied in blackstringed phylactery cubes among prayershawls & shrouds, this cockroach "dignity," this vein of coal gemlight "star," these ringworms "love" & "will," these trained vermin "courage" & "human," "honor" & "blame," god's burnished reichsmark "fate" (ashes to ashes), grapes from the vineyard "time," cheese stenchwedges of "spirit" & "faith," these dentures "choice" & "justice," these lead crystal compotes "story" & "poetry" (Aharon dreamed his mother/woke in her grave below the river) — all these to the warehouse, "Canada," that power to steal/stain/dispense/ divide/weld/wed each word, each aesthetic to its opposite, trancefragments, cargos of incoherence, rabbinical monocles of "vision" & "transcendence," this free & wild & incandescent history, human cattlefreightcar sounds vowelling across Europe with   all belongings, the Jews' exodus

up the chimneys.

Fallout

Shadows from History's "millennial" eclipse
Shatter and scatter
Throughout the stained-glass stratosphere
Enveloping this felon's Hell,
Irradiating the remaining population
With abstract shame and guilt,
Dusting streams, lakes, oceans, forests,
And cornfields with diseased spores,
Proliferating over all surfaces
Like advanced lymph-node cancer —
Earth's terminal prognosis!

A planet of thin-skinned survivors
Wobbles centrifugally
From its first eruption in Berlin,
Distorting memories of the Third Reich —
Its precise reason for existing
To commit cosmic crimes
Capable of extirpating an entire race;
Their brief rotation obscuring a defunct moon
Whose dying Jewish light
Became a very direct reflection
Of defective minds sinisterly inclined

To cast shadows on their own vast incredulity —
Who designed their Holocaust
As a heeltap to myriad earlier toasts
Raised to Thanatos:
Specters all, despite today's expiations,
Still stashing in mattresses and coal bins
"J"s and Stars of David
Their parents used for labeling vermin
And bequeathed them, just in case
Doomsday might come sooner than expected,
And they could goose-step in full uniform again;

But not without first belting schnapps
To screw their courage into boastful delusions
Of Aryan superiority over Jew, Man,
The stupefied planet, and God Himself;
Not without danse-ing macabre-ly
As its hot knot burns past epiglottis,
Rotting gut and collective Teutonic anus;
And not without defecating hydrocyanic waste
That will dust streams, lakes, oceans,
Cornfields, and forests, irradiating them
With Hell-spores, forever . . . forever . . . forever.

PART FOUR

Degrees in Bigotry

A New Bible

He told me his story, and today I have
forgotten it, but it was certainly a sorrowful,
cruel and moving story; because so are all our
stories, hundreds of thousands of stories, all
different and all full of tragic, disturbing
necessity. We tell them to each other in the
evening, and they take place in Norway, Italy,
Algeria, Ukraine, and are simple and incompre-
hensible like the stories in the Bible. But
are they not themselves stories of a new Bible?
—Primo Levi

Evening. A lamp glows softly, gives off barely enough light to read by. You and I are children, reading a book by the light of that lamp.

Our parents pass back and forth in front of us. The lamp shadows them against the walls.

We are reading a story from a new Bible. We are as quiet as the shadows.

In the story, a master orders the children to come to him. They leave their trains at a station where a clock is painted on false walls. It is always three o'clock. The master welcomes them. In two hours, at three o'clock, the children are ashes.

There is no end to this book. It begins again, with other stories, after its last page. The lamp seems to concentrate its light on our book.

In the yellow glow of the lamp on the pages of our story, we see other colors — mauve, rose. When we look up at the lampshade, we see erika blossoms, through which the bulb shines.

We turn the page. It is three o'clock. So many trains converge on the station, so many stories.

Waiting for Connecting Trains, 1983

Stranded in the bar of this rail-car restaurant,
Getting blitzed on dry Rhine wine,
I scream. Twilight shivers
As though a frigid blast has passed low
Or claws have scratched its back to bleeding
Below fog whirling like waves
Weaving into shore from deep-sea grottos.

Somehow, Cracow and Auschwitz drown vision
With dim intimidation;
My screams transfigure History into chimneys
Juden died in, rising, whose sacrifices
Hardly mattered, except as stench sullying the air —
Obliterated spirits assuming transcendence
Through involuntary "firing."

That vast disgrace shames me.
Hiding in this Victorian depot, I bellow,
But my presence goes unnoticed by cabaret whores
And blond, blue-eyed "*Jugend* boys"
Resembling in their proletarian arrogance
A confederacy of Grosz caricatures
Instead of students pursuing degrees in bigotry.

Finally my name is called; I stand
And am escorted into an adjoining boxcar for supper.
While I wait for someone to take my order,
My fingertips explore protruding rivets.
Suddenly this train lurches,
Clacks over tracks cast from fillings and rings
And laid on skeletons, not wooden ties.

Eating is a tribulation of enormous discomfort;
Salt drips from my eyes to my food.
Never would I have imagined
That each dish put before me, every libation,
Would take on Egyptian significance,
Become a Seder for a renegade
Unassimilated into the Final Solution,

Who never embraced orthodoxy, attended a synagogue,
Nor even practiced reform worship
Amidst hypocrisies of Jewish America,
But rather chose to remain a poet/ghost
Hymning his own *Kol Nidre*
From bunker and stalag to ghetto and slum
Along his lonely, self-imposed Diaspora.

Dinner finished, I return to the lounge
And witness twilight bleeding from stained-glass fanlights.
Like a fish twitching on a shore,
My drunken spirit quits its hallucinatory trip,
Passes out — but not before trying to refloat itself
In one more snifter. Through the distance
A locomotive's whistle bellows louder, louder.

The Trains

Signed by Franz Paul Stangl, Commandant,
there is in Berlin a document,
an order of transmittal from Treblinka:

248 freight cars of clothing,
400,000 gold watches,
25 freight cars of women's hair.

Some clothing was kept, some pulped for paper.
The finest watches were never melted down.
All the women's hair was used for mattresses, or dolls.

Would these words like to use some of that same paper?
One of those watches may pulse in your own wrist.
Does someone you know collect dolls, or sleep on human hair?

He is dead at last, Commandant Stangl of Treblinka,
but the camp's three syllables still sound like freight cars
straining around a curve, Treblinka,

Treblinka. Clothing, time in gold watches,
women's hair for mattresses and dolls' heads.
Treblinka. The trains from Treblinka.

Twilight

Only when he sits on his front stoop
Witnessing twilight drip blood
Does a tenacious sense of disillusionment
Infiltrate his defenses,
Rifle his desk, ransack his files,
And infect his mind with a hacker's virus
He knows will eventually blight
The entire pattern of historical events
He's spent a lifetime re-collecting,
Sequentially ordering,
Trying to explain and morally justify;
It's then he settles into a forlorn stupor.

His tongue-tied eyes glaze
As stomach and throat collaborate
In regurgitating the past
All over day's face and clothes,
Leaving a reeking pool of greenish drool
At Memory's feet in which he'll wallow all evening.
In dismal moments such as this,
He shivers like a stalked rabbit
Sensing a hunter has it in the focus
Of his thousand-power scope
And is about to nail it to a cross-hairs crucifix.
He quivers, as if back at Auschwitz,

Suspicioning these malevolent visions —
Issue of Scylla and Charybdis —
Lurk in a vortex beneath the surface,
Course between late afternoon and night
Where light and darkness
Disguise themselves as Life and Death,
Joy and Keening, Luck and Misfortune,
And play odd-man-out,
Each side hoping to survive the other's Fate.
Maybe what keeps reminding him he'd died
Are sunballs, like today's,
He recalls having first seen in '44

Through a crack in a boxcar door
As he rode the last transport leaving Sighet
For dislocations he'd call home
The rest of Destiny's trip.
He dies each time he sees from his porch
Twilight dripping blood
From night's great, gaping uterus
Or envisions a rusty, gushing sun at dusk
Spilling the shrill, stillborn fetuses
Of a million children of Zion,
Filling his nostrils with menstrual stench
From a womb-tomb at Earth's dead center.

Coin

What was a Jewish child worth, summer, 1944,
when the Nazis halved the dosage of *Zyklon B*
from 12 boxes to 6 boxes for each gassing?

When released, the gas rose, forcing the victims
in their death struggles to fight upward,
but the gas filled every pocket of air, at last.

What was a Jewish child worth when the Nazis,
to save money, doubled the agony
by halving the gas? 5 marks per kilogram,

5.5 kilograms invested in every Auschwitz chamberload
of 1500 units. With the mark at 25¢
this meant $6.75 per 1500 units,

or 45/100 of a cent per person. Still,
this was too much: sometimes the rationed gas
ran out during the long queue of consumers,

so children were thrown alive into the furnaces.
In the summer of 1944 at Auschwitz, a Jewish child
was not worth 1/2¢ to the Reich

which struck this coin, floating freely hellward now
into that economy, this twenty-five-mark piece,
one risked mark for each line, gas

for more than sixty children for each line,
if it please God and/or the Nazis in their mercy
to at least gas them before they are heaved

into the flames of the Thousand Year Reich.

Trevi Cabaret, 1944

In a Berlin bar, not far from the war,
I partake of transportations
The reeking darkness exhausts against my brain
Like feverish breath on a frozen windowpane.
A relentless blur disturbs vision;
I see naked Nazi ladies and gents
Writhing orgiastically on the dance floor,
Belly to belly to back,
Pretending to be down on their knees
Searching for lucky pennies —
Mirrored mosaics cascading from a globe
Spinning vertiginously above the klieg-lit stage —
With which to make their Jewish death wishes.

These glistening coins hover like dust motes
Just long enough
For the revelers to eye their mottos and dates,
Rub their eagles and wreathed swastikas
For old-fashioned, Teutonic luck
Before they fuse into musical pfennig-notes
And buy more whiskey and wine.
One by one, throughout the night,
I witness each toss his own dissolute profile
Over his left shoulder
And gaze vacantly as it spirals slowly,
Hopelessly to the bottom
Of the millennial Reich's Trevi-like delusion.

The Secret

The survivor spoke. I began to hear.
Not her cattlecar four eternal days from Budapest,
the dead buried under luggage in one corner —
I'd heard this before.
Not the shorning, the aberrant showers, the corpse stink of soup —
I'd heard this before.
Not the electrified barbed wire —
but as though her sentences
shorted themselves out,
phrases that buzzed & crackled
under her breastbone barracks. Not music,
the gaunt band playing the walking dead off to slave labor,
back from slave labor —
I'd heard this before, or tried to. But
red streaks of voice across
an ionized atmosphere,
gassed Hungarian clawhair & ribnails & tongues, a burst heart
breaking into static as she spoke,
into cancelling sparks,
her now never-ending speechlessness, never.

Incarnations of a Pawnbroker

How can a soul roam so far
Without making conversation with a friend
Or at least saying "Hello"
To a waif, hobo, or streetwalker
Somewhere along the road,
In a bar, alley, or beggar's graveyard?
How can a flown spirit,
No matter how wayward or dissociated,
Fail to make contact with his own shadow
Floating upwind from St. Louis,
Over New Haven and Haight-Ashbury,
And back to the Midwest, at rest in Katy Station?

I, the liberated poet my growing psyche
Always dreamed of becoming,
Almost to the exclusion of youthful goals —
Grades, girls, golden calves —
Ask myself these painful questions,
Hoping to resolve ambivalences
In which my private essence,
So temperamentally independent from the outset,
Now wallows.
Sitting here in this bar, bereft, invisible,
I listen into the distance
For the slightest feather falling from heaven

And pray Milton's archangel Michael
Will whisper in my ear
Intimations of God's nearness,
His commiseration for my diffidence.
Any answer that might justify my plight
Will be welcome tonight.
I'll make every allowance,
Forget precise tolerances I've used
To differentiate potential enemies from friends.
I'll even accept the sleaziest whore as my confidante,
Toast the first person daring enough
To share my loneliness.

Having been burned in Fate's furnace,
I can't recall my name, race, or place of birth.
To this day, a twisted, blue serial number,
Tattooed above my left wrist,
Is the only clue to my identity.
Horrifyingly, it makes me wonder
Whether, for more than forty years,
I've not been my own ghost,
Roaming back toward Lodz ghetto
To reunite with my truncated soul,
So abruptly dismissed
By the millennial Reich's misappropriation of History.

The Power

I signed my book   *Erika*   for a survivor
who told me her mother's name   Erika and

the platform at Auschwitz   freightcar
steaming and stinking behind them they

shuffled in line   toward   the immaculate one
Josef Mengele   in white   who   this time

distracted in business with another *SS* officer doctor
almost let them by   together   but

motioned them back   divided daughter for work
Erika   for her grave in the air   I

looked up   to the woman's daughter   who wore
a dress of wildflowers   Erika

with long black hair   here where
I hold the power   to let them leave freely   but

they must not trust me   not even
on the white page   where I could be   Mengele's

admirer   *you*   *to one side*   *you other*
join your ash mother   you

understand   I can't say but
Erika and   Erika's daughter they   walk away

though I could hold them   believe me   please
hurry   trust me I swear they

walk away   together   believe me I want them
to trust me   Jews   never

trust me I'll keep   talking   tell them
to keep walking   away   tell them   please

trust me   never   tell them
schnell   run   tell them   believe me   hurry . . .

Crying Wolf for the Last Time

Tonight, sleeping under soiled, freezing sheets
In his drafty tenement,
He's assailed by a dizzy, persistent vision
From a traditional fairy tale
Whose surreal images his memory has transfigured
Into mocking, idiotic shapes and shrill sounds
That cloud dreams in shrouds of restive doubt.

Unable to submit to amniotic solemnity,
He witnesses all too disturbingly
Three meek, little Yiddish piggies
Shivering from the specter of their hairy adversary,
The big, bad, Hitlerian wolf;
Three porcine victims squealing hysterically,
Huddled in fearful anguish and ignominious despair,

Listening to the goose-stepping, lupine beast
Thrashing through the dry thatching
Of their ghetto-shelter's roof.
Terrified of his feeding frenzy,
They realize too soon he'll violate them,
Not by huffing, puffing, and blowing curses
At their verminous dwelling,

But rather by sliding down their chimney,
That indefensible opening
Through which he'll arrive head first
Or breech, on his feet,
The better to leap, rip their throats
With ravenous teeth, devour them,
Leaving only their Kosher bones,

Then race out the door
To a biergarten near Oswiecim Forest
Where he'll quench his burning thirst
And mate with a bosomy she-wolf
For a few indolent hours
Before marching back into History,
Down Valhalla's witnessless corridors.

Although in past catastrophes
His imagination has been extremely inventive,
Tonight it can't alchemize from Nightmare
Even an excrement pot
Those porkers might fill with boiling water
To entrap an unwitting Lupus
As it descends their constricted flue.

Preternaturally, Sleep's logs he saws
Ignite in a fireplace into whose flames
He sees the three piggies leap
And bake to unsavory crisps
Before disappearing up the brick chimney, —
Their only escape from the predacious wolf —
Spiraling so high into the star-scarred sky

Their ashes are annealed in its *Yahrzeit* glow.

PART FIVE

Our Star

Wind-Chill Factors

Lublin, Vilna, Grodno, Bialystok, Lodz,
Warsaw, Cracow, Lvov,
The rivers San, Vistula, and Bug,
And so many more names, just names,
He rips from his tongue's tip
Like a vicious wind snapping icicles
This blisteringly frigid, snowy morning
Three days before Christmas.
(Or is it four?)

Dallying in his café at 5:00 a.m.,
Waiting for regulars to arrive,
He idly sips freshly brewed coffee
And gazes at steam rising from its surface,
Clouded with iridescent acid patches
Resembling human ash.
Its heat doesn't thaw his blood,
And he knows it won't, either,
As long as he sees smoke, not vapors,

Sees the cracked mug
As an active, black chimney stack,
Sees human fat crackling in mass graves
Instead of liquid sloshing in a cup.
Damn! Why is it
That on winter days like this one,
Especially around Christmas,
He fixes on this litany,
As if reciting Polish names from his youth

Might mitigate terrible paranoias?
And how did he, Carl Czarnecki,
A fifty-two-year-old Jewish cook,
Somehow find his way to St. Louis
In '44 or '45 and stay?
Why should he see images of Death
He never even knew firsthand
And, by pure Aryan chance, eluded
When he was six or seven or Methuselahan?

➡

Lublin, Vilna, Grodno, Bialystok, Lodz,
Warsaw, Cracow, Lvov, etc.;
Names, just Eastern European names
Of towns, cities, rivers, and regions —
Ah, but also those other names,
So close yet so sinisterly remote
With their hideously idiosyncratic odors and moans:
Belzec, Chelmno, Bergen-Belsen,
Auschwitz-Birkenau;

Names that on blisteringly frigid days
Like this (the radio warns
The wind chill will hit sixty below),
Numb his toes, chatter his teeth,
Keep his eyelids twitching,
Though coffee he'll swill all day
Scalds his tongue and stomach.
Suddenly someone commands, "Hey, waiter!"
He snaps to attention and salutes.

The Apple

I

In Israel at that time just after the war,
we did not have much to eat,
so when, at the beach, I saw an apple bobbing in the waves,
glistening red, far out, but an apple for sure,
I swam for it.

I did reach the object,
and, as I'd thought, it was an apple.
I carried it to shore in my bosom,
thinking of its juice and firm flesh.
But, inside, it was rotten:

it had been thrown from a boat,
or a cloud, for good reason.
Were you to eat a bit of my survivor's heart
even the size of an apple seed,
it would poison you.

II

In Israel at that time just after the war,
we did not have much to eat,
so when, at the beach, I saw an apple bobbing in the waves,
glistening red, far out, but an apple for sure,
I swam for it.

I did reach the object,
but it was not an apple.
Unbelievable as this might be, it was an eye,
perhaps from an octopus, or a shark,
or a whale, but an eye,

translucid red, a watery gel,
its pupil black and unmistakable.
Perhaps this was the eye of the angel
of the camps. I cupped it in my hands.
I swallowed at least one mouthful, to see.

Man's Best Friend

These days, he barely escapes gnashing teeth
Of hallucinatory intruders on his sleep.
He awakens before dawn each morning
To lice and scabies inspection
By sycophantish *Kapos*,
Collaborators of his tormented dreams,
Assigned to systematically subjugate him.
He wears despair over his bones like flesh,
Speaks a mixture of Yiddish,
Russian, English, and Italian
In response to commands he can't understand.

Staring into the mirror above the basin,
He recalls how his brown hair
Turned gray overnight
When he'd hid in the latrine,
Submerged up to his neck in dreck,
Waiting for guards to vacate the dark yard
So he could follow his instincts
Away from Oswiecim;
He shakes his head as if to reset connections
Between eyes and memory
But doesn't recognize his vacant reflection.

Next, he routinely uncages his sole companion,
A black cocker spaniel
He's never been able to name;
Inextricably leashed, they go outside
To the place where, with wide sweeps
And feigned disinterest, it initiates its ritual circling.
Waiting patiently while it sniffs, nuzzles roots,
Chews grass, he anticipates contractions
Just beneath its stubby tail,
And counting, piece by piece, cylindrical feces
Sliding out its ass, shares vicariously

In its relief. The thorough earth
Accepts its sacrificial offerings.
Suddenly his dog metamorphoses
Into a million Jewish children and adults
Who, having already sullied clothes and skin
In the hot, putrescent boxcars
Lacking even an excrement pot,
Are yet stooping beside train tracks
Between "home" and the sinister Unknown,
Desperately urinating and relieving their bowels;
Dignified Jew-dogs who, until days before,

Had never known canines could dream,
Remember, grieve, fear,
And hear Death near enough to smell it,
Nor ever imagined they might see themselves
Publicly perform bodily acts,
Let alone with such animal shamelessness.
Watching his spaniel with insane fascination,
He squats sympathetically,
Unconscious of possible disapprobation
From neighbors he's never met
Or spoken to — not even to say "Hello."

For a moment, he can almost feel the weight
Entire generations of Jews
Placed on the thighs of the German nation
As it strained to shit out its bleeding anus
Those it depended on for nourishment.
Why his days begin and end this way
He can't guess, except that without his dog,
He knows he'd be even lonelier.
Maybe walking his pet reminds him
It's time to clean out Memory's latrine
And climb inside again.

The Numinous

Our language has no term that can
isolate distinctly and gather into one
word the total numinous impression a
thing may make on the mind.
— Rudolf Otto

We are walking a sidewalk
in a German city.
We are watching gray smoke
gutter along the roofs
just as it must have
from other terrible chimneys.
We are walking our way
almost into a trance.
We are walking our way
almost into a dream
only those with blue
numbers along their wrists
can truly imagine.

Now, just in front of us, something
bursts into the air.
For a few moments
our bodies echo fear.
Pigeons, we say,
only an explosion
of beautiful blue-gray pigeons.
Only pigeons that gather
over the buildings
and begin to circle.

We are walking again, counting
all the red poinsettias
between the windowpanes
and lace curtains.
It was only
a flock of pigeons:
we can still see them
circling over the block buildings,
a hundred hearts
beating in the air.
Beautiful blue-gray pigeons.
We will always remember.

Gestapo Crows

I

This crisp Sunday a.m.,
He slips out his front door,
Undetected *almost*, tiptoes into brittleness
As though, somehow, it mattered.
In fact, he lives alone.
His only witnesses are crows
Clotted in the tops of phlebitic oaks,
Higher than his vision goes.

Perhaps the ferocious cawing he hears
Comes from a hundred lusting predators
Coveting the steaming, crimson guts
Of a sundered squirrel
Impaled on a limb above him.
Poised on his porch stoop, he shivers;
Most likely, it's October's raptorial winds
That are clawing his throat raw.

Uncertain whether to leave in his auto
Or withdraw, he pauses;
Vacillation may be the brain's way
Of recalibrating Thought's train schedules
To allow troop-transports open track
While freights hauling Jew-cattle stall,
Back up, overflow Hades' yards.
His lapse goes unrecorded,

Except by three crows
Violently lurching from perches atop his chimney
Like smoky, black cloud-ghosts
Swerving toward the source of primordial screeching.
Nervously he senses that his quivering
Is intimately coincident
With those grotesquely vociferous, bellicose birds;
He slips indoors before they smell him.

II

For a decade before the '36 Olympics
Were played out in Berlin,
He'd seen Europe's Jews running distances,
Practicing wind sprints
To compete in the Great Aryan Marathon
Judged by the Master Race Committee;
He'd felt their Achilles' tendons flexing,
Stretching past elasticity,
Heard them snap with a thwack so plangent
No spectator could have escaped that Accident:
He'd come away with a sympathetic limp.

Almost half a century after he fled Leipzig,
Obscene crows still huddle in his oaks,
Waiting for the Jew below
To break from his St. Louis ghetto;
Cloaking their Gestapo uniforms
Beneath trench coats of sleek, jet feathers,
They keep systematic vigil
To make certain he doesn't, once again,
Elude the Führer's *dushegubka*
(Exterminator and hearse under one roof)
Or "Jew down" Fate with his usurer's tongue.

They clot in the top limbs like festering scabs,
Flutter hysterically from tree to tree
Like human puffs spewing out Memory's chimneys.
Always, when sneaking from his house
To buy supplies he relies on to resist the Enemy,
That old dread overwhelms him:
He sees those predatory crows,
So terribly arrogant in their contrariness,
Talons bared, wings spread wide,
Diving, pecking him in his Achilles' heel,
Pecking him bloody, pecking him to death.

III

While out jogging the newly paved streets
Stitching his pre-war subdivision,
He passed a mashed squirrel
And, coming to a complete stop,
Gaped at its eyeless left socket,
Teeth collapsed in its jaws' gnawed gums,
And bleeding anus and genitals
Crows' beaks were still drilling as he approached.

Even now, fleeing the City in his auto,
He recollects the grotesqueness
Of those six or eight strutting black crows
Ripping that creature into confetti
Right under his nose — such rapaciousness
Unheeded by squirrels importunately foraging,
Digging, burying nuts, storing up
Against winter's death-echoes.

Driving westerly, he can't eradicate the horror
Those oversized scavengers evoked
Or forget the obliviousness those rodents showed
Toward the en-crow-ching Enemy:
Everything so seemingly undisturbed, except to him.
Suddenly he recalls that attitude of smugness
His Jewish community boasted
In its almost goading, "Chosen" insularity,

Proclaiming itself inviolable
Back in '38,
Even as the Reich's circling eagle
Had spied them and was flexing to dive,
Just prior to his fleeing Leipzig for Holland,
Ellis Island, eventually St. Louis,
Where, to this day, he's been in hiding
Despite assurances of the Führer's cyanide-suicide.

The Candle

It would do me no good to travel to Auschwitz.
It would do the dead no good, nor anyone else any good.
It would do me no good to kneel there,
me nor anyone else alive or dead any good, any good at all.

I've heard that in one oven a votive candle
whispers its flame. When I close my eyes,
I can see and feel that candle, its pitch aura,
its tongues of pitch luminescence licking the oven's recesses.

A survivor, forty years later, crawled up into an oven and lay down.
What of his heart? Could it keep pumping its own pitch light
here where God's human darkness grew darkest?
Whoever you were, please grant me dispensation.

Rudolf Hess praised the efficiency of these ovens.
It would do me no good to travel to Auschwitz, to kneel or lie down.
It would do me or God or anyone else alive or dead,
or anyone else neither alive nor dead no good, no good at all.

The survivor did crawl back out of the oven.
He took his heart with him, didn't he not, it kept beating.
He left his heart in the oven, and it keeps beating, black-black,
black-black, the candle of the camps.

Eyes closed, staring up into this, eyebeams of pitch luminescence,
and the pulse of it, the heart, the candle — you and I,
haven't we not, have met him, the one who lay himself down there
where the Nazis had missed some, welcome, welcome home. . . .

We have spoken the candle heart of the camps.
It does the dead no good, nor us any good, doesn't it not,
but it keeps, black-black, its watch of pitch light,
and will. Any good at all. Wouldn't we not? The candle.

Survivor

For William Heyen

His inconspicuous disappearance from the City
Is nothing less or more
Than the feckless non sequitur of deaf-mutes
Debating the existential ethics of silence.
Fleeing is his tongue-tied expression of freedom,
Meek gesture of abnegation,
Civil disobedience à la Gandhi and Thoreau,
His microcosmic vote for Anarchy of the Soul.

O, what a timorous milquetoast he appears
Squinting back at himself,
Scowling skeptically at his distorted reflection
In the rearview mirror
He keeps focused in front of himself
To avoid Maginot-line surprises
From enemies encroaching on his blind side,
Mind-parasites and vermin-worms

Sucking dry his hope of escaping undetected
Time's elusive "private eyes."
Poor bastard! There's never a moment's rest
From his paranoic surveillance,
Never a fresh breath, brief respite,
Nor pause from the Cause Célèbre!
Always, it's another quixotic decision
To make a dash for it,

As if no-man's-land between birth and death
Were measured in highway miles
Rather than by degrees of loneliness so deep
No one who submits
Recognizes himself on returning from its abyss.
Always, he seems just on the verge
Of discovering the purpose of purposelessness
When arriving awakens him to his dream,

And he's forced to submit to inspection
By border-patrol soldiers,
Lie naked, legs spread
While frothing Doberman pinschers
Sniff his anus, lick his shriveled genitals.
He's never eluded this hallucination
Or the other one of burning alive
In an oven *Sonderkommandos* have been stoking

Since 1945, when Patton's Third Army
Liberated his disembodied spirit
Seconds before he'd have been baked into matzo
For Hitler's last Seder.
Today's trip out from St. Louis
Is no different from his very first ride
Via freight train from Berlin
To a place whose name still makes him quake.

The Children

I do not think we can save them.
I remember, within my dream, repeating
I do not think we can save them.
But our cars follow one another
over the cobblestones. Our dim
headlamps, yellow in fog, brush past,
at the center of a market square,
its cathedral's great arched doors.
I know, now, this is a city
in Germany, two years
after the Crystal Night. I think ahead
to the hospital, the children.
I do not think we can save them.

Inside this dream,
in a crystal dashboard vase,
one long-stemmed rose unfolds
strata of soft red light.
Its petals fall, tears, small
flames. I cup my palm to hold them,
and my palm fills to its brim,
will overflow.
Is this the secret, then? . . .
Now I must spill the petal light, and drive.

We are here, in front of the hospital,
our engines murmuring. Inside,
I carry a child under each arm,
down stairs, out to my car.
One's right eyeball hangs on its cheek
on threads of nerve and tendon,
but he still smiles, and I love him.
The other has lost her chin —
I can see straight down her throat
to where her heart beats
black-red, black-red.
I do not think we can save them.

I am the last driver in this procession.
Many children huddle in my car.
We have left the city. Our lights
tunnel the fog beneath arches of linden,
toward Bremerhaven, toward
the western shore.
I do not think we can save them.
This time, at the thought, lights
whirl in my mirror, intense
fear, and the screams of sirens.
I begin to cry, for myself, for the children.
A voice in my dream says
this was the midnight you were born. . . .

Later, something brutal happened, of course,
but as to this life I had to, I woke,
and cannot, or will not, remember.
But the children, of course, were murdered,
their graves lost, their names lost,
even those two faces lost to me. Still,
this morning, inside the engine of my body,
for once, as I wept and breathed deep,
relief, waves of relief, as though the dreamed

rose would spill its petals forever.
I prayed thanks. For one night, at least,
I tried to save the children,
to keep them safe in my own body,
and knew I would again. Amen.

A Barren Marriage

Two human survivors of the Holocaust,
Jewess and Jew,
Beautiful to each other,
Blessed keepers of the imperishable faith
That humored Pharaoh and Hitler,
Share a heritage of enduring frailty,

Squeeze each other in a breathless embrace
Millennially deep. They believe
Their impassioned arteries and veins,
Sympathetically pulsating,
Draining and refilling ancient reservoirs,
Circulate the entire fated history of their race.

In naked view of the ascending moon,
They tongue Dead Sea fluids
To quench their cells' thirst for salt,
Renew menstrual cycles halted in the camps;
Then, gently blending egg and sperm,
They pray they'll create a child

Who just might survive them
Into a future when Gentile and Jew,
Moslem, Buddhist, and Hindu
Will kiss each others' exotic lips
Without offending anyone's God;
And always they fall asleep hoping, hoping.

This Night

Which is our star this night?
Belsen is bathed in blue,
every footworn lane, every
strand of wire, pale blue.
The guards' bodies,
the prisoners' bodies — all
black and invisible. Only
their pale blue eyes
float above the lanes
or between the wires.
Or they are all dead,
and these are the blue eyes of those
haunted by what happened here.
Which eyes are yours,
which mine? Even
blue-eyed crows
drift the darkness overhead. Even
blue-eyed worms
sip dew from the weeping leaves
of the black Erika
over the graves. . . .
But now, at once, every
eye, every blue light
closes. As we do.
For rest. For now.
Which was our star this night?

LOUIS DANIEL BRODSKY

My poems in this volume have their collective origin in my
Imagination; they have appeared over the past few years as surreal,
if all-too-real, agents of evil, despair, and hope. They were not
conceived as dramatic renditions nor interpretations of oral or
published accounts by victims, refugees, their children, or
historians of the Holocaust, but rather as poetic "intuitive
recollections" necessarily registered by a second-generation
"survivor" who refuses to ignore, deny, repress, or forget history.
As such, I claim full responsibility for their "accuracy" and
"authenticity."

Certain of my poems originally carried the names of persons to
whom they were dedicated; although they don't appear in this
publication, I should like to acknowledge them now:

"Lovesong" — For Julius Lester

"For the Time Being" — For Harry James Cargas

"Liberation from Buchenwald" — For Elie Wiesel

"Himmler at Auschwitz, 1942" — For Sanford Budick

"Twilight" — For Elie Wiesel

"A Barren Marriage" — For Jane Goldberg

WILLIAM HEYEN

"Men in History": Much of this poem is based on Albert Speer's memoir *Inside the Third Reich* (New York, 1970).

"Children's Poem: This Village": Irving Greenberg mentions this village in his essay "Cloud of Smoke, Pillar of Fire: Judaism, Christianity, and Modernity after the Holocaust," in *Auschwitz: Beginning of a New Era? Reflections on the Holocaust*, ed. Eva Fleischner (New York, 1977).

"Kotov": I've been unable to relocate the book in which I found the history of Ivanovitch Kotov, but his story is a true one.

"The Lice Boy of Belsen": Hanna Levy-Hass in her *Inside Belsen* (Totowa, N.J., 1982) tells of one such victim.

"A Professor of Mathematics": Robert Skloot's *The Darkness We Carry: The Drama of the Holocaust* (Madison, Wis., 1988) contains a letter that relates this incident.

"Sonnet and Haiku: Forms from the Reich University": My poem is based on a letter quoted in *Remember Nuremberg*, by A. Poltorak and Y. Zaitsev (Moscow, n.d.).

"Poem Touching the Gestapo": The epigraphs are from Edward Crankshaw's *Gestapo* (New York, 1956) and Olga Lengyel's *Five Chimneys* (St. Albans, Hertfordshire, 1972).

"Scripture: Himmler on Mercilessness": I drew on the excerpt from Himmler's speech used by Jean-Francois Steiner as an epigraph to *Treblinka* (New York, 1968).

"Canada": For some reason unknown to me "Canada" was the name given to a huge warehouse-dispensary-collection center at Auschwitz.

"A New Bible": The epigraph from Primo Levi is from his *If This is Man* (New York, 1959). It was at Treblinka where a clock whose hands pointed to three was painted on a false wall at the arrival "station."

"Coin": I've taken the statistics in this poem from Irving Greenberg's essay (see note above to "Children's Poem: This Village").

"The Apple": The first part of this poem is based on an anecdote told to Helen Epstein in her *Children of the Holocaust: Conversations with Sons and Daughters of Survivors* (New York, 1979).

"The Numinous": The epigraph is from Otto's *The Idea of the Holy*, translated by John W. Harvey (New York, 1958).

Louis Daniel Brodsky was born in St. Louis, Missouri, in 1941, where he attended St. Louis Country Day School. After earning a B.A., Magna Cum Laude, at Yale University in 1963, he received an M.A. in English from Washington University in 1967 and an M.A. in Creative Writing from San Francisco State University the following year.

From 1968 until 1987, while maintaining his writing schedule, he managed a 350-person men's clothing factory and developed a chain of "Slack Outlets" for Biltwell Co., Inc. of St. Louis, Missouri.

Mr. Brodsky is the author of fifteen volumes of poetry. In addition, he has published eight scholarly books on Nobel laureate William Faulkner, and most recently, a biography titled *William Faulkner, Life Glimpses*.

Listing his occupation as Poet, he is also Curator of the Brodsky Faulkner Collection at Southeast Missouri State University in Cape Girardeau, Missouri.

William Heyen's poems have appeared in more than a hundred periodicals, including *The New Yorker, Harper's, TriQuarterly, Poetry,* and *American Poetry Review.* His honors include two fellowships from the National Endowment for the Arts, the John Simon Guggenheim Fellowship in Poetry, the Eunice Tietjens Memorial Prize from *Poetry* magazine, and the Witter Bynner Prize for Poetry from the American Academy and Institute of Arts and Letters. Mr. Heyen's previous books include **Depth of Field, Long Island Light, Lord Dragonfly,** and **Erika: Poems of the Holocaust,** fast becoming a classic of its kind. His next volume of poetry, **Pterodactyl Rose: Poems on Ecology,** as well as a second edition of **Erika,** are forthcoming from his permanent publisher, Timeless Press of St. Louis, Missouri. Mr. Heyen is currently Professor of English and Poet in Residence at the State University of New York College at Brockport.

More Great American Poetry
available from
Time Being Books: Poetry in Sight and Sound

LOUIS DANIEL BRODSKY

You Can't Go Back, Exactly

The Thorough Earth

Four and Twenty Blackbirds Soaring

Mississippi Vistas: Volume One of *A Mississippi Trilogy*

Mistress Mississippi: Volume Two of *A Mississippi Trilogy*

Forever, for Now: Poems for a Later Love

A Gleam in the Eye: Poems for a First Baby
Volume One of *A Pentalogy of Childhood*

WILLIAM HEYEN

Erika: Poems of the Holocaust

Pterodactyl Rose: Poems of Ecology

Please call or write for a free catalog.

TIME BEING BOOKS
POETRY IN SIGHT AND SOUND
Saint Louis, Missouri

10411 Clayton Road • Suite 208
St. Louis, Missouri 63131
(314) 432-1771

TO ORDER TOLL-FREE
(800) 331-6605 Monday through Friday, 8 a.m. to 4 p.m. Central time
FAX: (314) 432-7939